Cattywampus Christmas

A "Nameless, Texas" Comedy

by Bobbi A. Chukran

From the Prize-Winning Stage Play
*"Dot and the (Amazing Technicolor)
Quest for the Real Santa Clause"*

Limestone Ledge Publishing

Taylor, Texas

Copyright © 2014 by Bobbi A. Chukran

All rights reserved. No part of this book may be reproduced in any form or by any electronic or mechanical means including information storage and retrieval systems, except in the case of brief quotations in critical reviews or articles, without permission in writing from the publisher. The characters, locations and events in this book are a product of the author's imagination and are used fictitiously. Any similarity to real persons, living or dead, is purely coincidental and not intended by the author.

ISBN: 978-0-944577-13-4

First paperback edition: November 2014

Cover Art by Bobbi A. Chukran

Also available in e-book formats.

Dedication

For Daddy, with love.
I still miss you every single day.

Cast of Characters

Dorothy Norton—AKA "Dot." Young woman who comes back to her parent's home for Christmas and falls into a crazy adventure.

Doris Morris—Dot's aunt. Crazy, but lovable.

Nancy Lee Norton—Dot's mother

John Parker—A neighbor who needs to practice his driving skills

Cattywampus Bonaparte—Formerly stuffed toy cat brought to life. Sassy fellow. A cheeky monkey.

Bo Raggley—The rag doll. Fashionista wannabe. Meek and mild.

Robot—Rusty old toy with hidden skills.

Herman Elf—A very rude fellow who needs to learn some manners.

Mrs. Santa Clause—Needs no introduction. She's keeping it all together.

Santa Clause—This is NOT the Santa of your childhood, believe me.

CATTYWAMPUS CHRISTMAS

CHAPTER ONE

A few days before Christmas, Dorothy Norton opened the front door of her parent's ranch-style house in Nameless, Texas and peeked her head around the corner. "Knock, knock! Anybody home?" She called out as she entered, pulling a large suitcase behind her. "Don't shoot, it's just me, Dot!"

Dot walked in, pulled the door shut then stopped and looked around the room. The furniture looked the way it always did, with the threadbare sofa covered with a brightly crocheted afghan and her dad's old recliner sitting in the corner. A fire crackled in the red brick fireplace. A mediocre painting of a field of bluebonnets hung on the wall beside the door. The smell of pine filled the air.

The old furniture was the only thing that looked familiar. Everything else seemed a bit strange.

Raucous music was blaring on the stereo. Dot listened for a moment, and then finally identified *Glow Worm* by Rockapella. She thought it was a strange choice for her country-western music-loving mother. Hank Williams, Sr. was more her speed. Dot walked over and turned down the volume. "Mama? It's me, Dot. Are you home?"

She wandered around, taking in the rest of the room. It had been decorated to the hilt for the holidays. The tallest Christmas tree she had ever seen sat back in the corner by the fireplace. It must have been six-feet wide at the base, and it almost reached the ceiling at the top.

The branches shook and a hand, then an arm, then Nancy Lee Norton, Dot's mother, emerged from the middle of it.

"We're over here, dear!" she called. "We didn't expect you for a few days."

The tree quivered again, and Dot's aunt, Doris Morris, emerged with her eyeglasses askew and her upswept hairdo halfway down into her eyes.

She pulled Dot into a choking embrace. "Hello, sweetheart! It's so good to see you."

Dot laughed and squirmed to break free. "I left work early and thought I'd surprise y'all. You know how I love Christmas. I couldn't wait to get back home and help you with all the decorations and shopping. I really missed you guys!" she said, rushing over to hug her mother.

"So, what do you think?" her mother asked, sweeping her arms around the room like an over-caffeinated game show hostess. "Nice, huh?"

Dot walked around slowly, taking in the decorations. The room was decked out like an upscale hotel lobby with everything modern—all in black, purple and lime green. A huge wreath the size of a wagon wheel hung above the fireplace and was decorated with black and purple ornaments topped off with a huge lime and white polka dot bow. A string of garland hanging over the front of the fireplace was also festooned with purple glass ornaments.

Dot stared in dismay, but tried to think of something to say that wouldn't hurt her mother's feelings. "Wow, looks like you've already done all the decorating. And it looks so . . . modern. And fancy. Not like you at all, to tell the truth." Sort of like you're decorating for Halloween, she thought.

Her mother smiled. "Yes! I know! Don't you love it? We just couldn't wait to get busy. We started decorating the day after Halloween, transitioned right past Falloween, on through Thanksgiving and are headed right smack dab into Christmas!"

"Once we got going, there was no stoppin' us!" Doris explained. "Me and your mama were just a couple of crazy whirlin' dervish decorators!" She flung her hands up, twirled then collapsed on the sofa. "Whew! We've had a bit of eggnog, dear," she explained. "To help the process along."

"I see," Dot said. "I'm sorry I wasn't here before now. I tried to get away for Thanksgiving but my boss refused to let me have the time off. So many stores were open on the holiday to catch the early shoppers."

Her mother shrugged. "Oh that's all right. Nobody pays attention to Thanksgiving much anymore around here. It's just a big ol' meal in between Halloween and Christmas with way too much football and people stuffing their faces with food. Big nuisance, you ask me."

"Your mother and I wanted to surprise you and get most of the decorating done before you got home. So—how do you like it?" Dot's aunt asked.

"Well, it's definitely, uh, different. Not old-fashioned at all," Dot admitted. "And certainly not what I expected from you two."

"Exactly! Out with the old, I say."

Doris clapped her hands. "And in with the new! I told you she'd love it, Nancy Lee."

Dot's mother rolled her eyes. "Yes, you were right. Once again."

Dot laughed then glanced around. "Where's Daddy? Out in the workshop?"

Her mother flapped her wrists. "Oh, I don't know, off down the road somewhere, if I had to guess. Our giant inflatable helicopter with Santa inside got loose in the windstorm last night and blew all over kingdom come. I guess he's still out trying to track it down."

"You have an inflatable helicopter? Wow. I thought you hated Christmas yard decorations," Dot said. She remembered the hissy fit her mother had thrown the year before when the neighbor put up their revolving twelve-foot snowman. She complained that the noise from the air compressor and the singing elves kept her awake all night. Not to mention the red flashing reindeer eyes that looked like aliens.

"Well, everybody has them now, dear. I didn't want the neighbors to think we weren't making an effort. Nameless, Texas is getting chic!" Her mother looked at her watch and frowned. "Your father should have been back by now, though."

Doris shook her head. "I TOLD him and TOLD him to tether that dag-blasted thing down with a couple of cement blocks! But he never listens to me! I hope it didn't land in Mr. Parker's backyard. He'll poke holes in it with his pitchfork for spite if it lands in his garden."

"Well, your brother never listens to me, either, and I'm his wife!"

"Truer words were never spoken, Nancy Lee. Although, sometimes I do have to take his side. For example, there was that time you . . ."

Dot decided to change the subject before things got out of hand. "When are y'all going Christmas shopping? I waited to do all of mine because it's always such an adventure going with you two! We're gonna have such fun this week!"

"Sorry, honey, my shopping's done!" Doris said, symbolically dusting her hands together. "Done AND done! Over with! Finished, even!"

Dot's mother nodded. "So is mine! I got tired of all that mess and hassle. Last year I shopped online, and it took forever! I saved a lot of time this year by getting the cute little plastic gift cards for everybody. Have you seen those? They're so cute! And they come in so many different designs, too. I sent sister Roseanne a Target gift card, and sent Mama a Wal-marts gift card. I just slipped them in with my annual Christmas newsletter. It was so easy and I didn't have to stand in line at the post office. I tell you what, that was a big weight off of my mind!"

"What did Sister and Mama give you last year? I can't remember," Doris asked.

"Hmmm, let me think," Dot's mother said. "I think Roseanne sent me a Wal-Marts gift card, and Mama sent me an Office Depot gift card."

"Office Depot? How . . .odd," Dot mumbled, but her mother ignored her.

"What did you end up buying with those?" Doris asked.

"I saved them and bought some house shoes for Mama's birthday with the gift card Roseanne sent me, and I bought some stationery for Roseanne's birthday with the gift card Mama sent me."

Dot frowned. "Mother! Honestly! That's so . . . boring! You bought gift cards for everybody this year?"

Her mother nodded. "I sure did. Besides, it's green to give gift cards. Eco-friendly! You save on wrapping paper and boxes and all sorts of stuff. AND they are so easy to mail so that cuts down on postal energy costs!"

Dot's aunt sniffed. "But they ARE plastic, Nancy Lee. Can't forget that. Plastic is NOT green."

Her mother's face turned red. "What are you now, Doris, the eco-police? Besides, I'm sure they're made from recycled plastic."

"Just sayin'," Doris smirked, then turned to Dot. "What do you want for Christmas this year?"

"Really? Let's see, I'll have some world peace, an end to global warming and I want more government subsidies for small family farms," Dot said. "And warm homes for all the stray animals. I'm pretty sure there aren't gift cards for those, though," she added.

Her mother laughed. "You are such a cut-up! Seriously, what do you really want? I can get you a gift card if you want to pick out something for yourself. How about a coffee shop card? That would save me a lot of time since there's one on every street corner around here. You do drink that hideous stuff, don't you? Everybody your age seems to be addicted to it."

"You don't have to buy me anything, mama," Dot said. "I don't need anything else. I can't keep up with dusting all the stuff I have now. And for what it's worth, I can't stand that nasty coffee. It tastes like that vile liquid Daddy used to boil in an old aluminum pot on the stove."

Her mother nodded. "Oh yes, I remember that. Egods, that was rank! I wonder how we all survived it. At least he's graduated to a Mr. Coffee by now. And organic home-ground beans," she added.

"Now, Dot, you have to let us buy you something. It wouldn't be right if we didn't," Doris explained. "It wouldn't be Christmas."

"It would be anti-American if we didn't buy you something," her mother said. "Think of the economy, dear."

"I don't want you to spend your hard-earned money on me. I have all the stuff I need," Dot said.

Her mother laughed. "Oh, that's all right, I'll just put it on the credit cards. I haven't maxed them ALL out yet. And they keep sending me new ones! Your father hides them from me, but then I open the mail and there's another one! It's amazing, just like magic!"

For a moment, Dot pondered the irony of buying plastic gift cards with plastic credit cards. She shook her head and decided to change the subject—again.

She sniffed the air and frowned. There was definitely something missing. "How come I don't smell food cooking? I thought y'all would be as busy as little elves in the kitchen. Are you going to make your famous Date Nut Cake? I love that cake! I save up my calories all year just so I can eat your cake at Christmas time. That caramel icing should be illegal, it's so good! I'm sure the smell alone is worth a couple of calories."

Her mother shook her head. "Oh, we decided not to bother with cooking this year. We're all going out to Do-Lolly's Diner for their annual turkey dinner feast, then we're coming home and vegging out. Maybe we'll watch an old movie on the TV. I think they're showing The Wizard of Oz again. Remember watching that when you were young? We saw it every year around Christmas-time."

Dot frowned. "You're kidding about the food, right?"

"Nope," her aunt and mother chorused, simultaneously.

"We took a vote and made a unanimous decision. Besides, nobody wants to mess with all those dishes," Doris admitted. "Or leftovers. Of course, there are paper plates, but those aren't very eco-friendly, are they?"

Her mother smiled. "But if you want the real smell of Christmas, I did buy some vanilla sugar cookie scented candles, and some Scent-o-the-Holidays oils that you spray on the tree to make it seem real."

Dot remembered the smell of pine as she'd walked in the door. "So the tree's not real?"

"Oh, mercy no!" her mother exclaimed. "We don't want all those messy needles all over the floor, sticking to the bottom of our shoes to track all over the house, getting ground down into the rugs. These new trees are much nicer, and so perfectly shaped."

Dot stared at the tree. It was perfect. A little too perfect, like only a plastic tree could be. "Have I been plopped down in Oz, or something? I don't know who y'all are anymore. Where is my real mother? What have you done with my aunt? I don't belong here. Maybe I'd better go back outside and check the address on the door."

Dot's mother laughed. "Nonsense! You're just tired from that long drive," she said. "The long drive that you had to make by yourself," she added.

Dot flushed. "Mother! Please, don't start. I'm perfectly happy with my life. Sure, I get a bit lonely now and then, but I have my work, and my friends."

"Oh, leave her alone, Nancy Lee," Doris said. "She'll settle down when she's ready. Come on, let's get this tree finished."

"You're right. Now, where were we?" Dot's mother stared at the tree for a moment, hopped back up on the ladder and her sister-in-law handed ornaments up to her.

"It needs more of those black balls on the right hand side there," Doris said, pointing to the top of the tree. "No, higher, no, lower. No! More in-between. Down a little. There, you got it!"

Dot's mother looked around, frowning. "Do you see my Elvis ornament there in that box? I cannot have Christmas without my Elvis ornament. Uncle Willie gave that to me right before he passed. It's genuine hand-blown glass. Luckily, Elvis is wearing a purple and black pantsuit, so it matches our color theme."

Doris winked at Dot. "I didn't know they had glass way back then."

"Very funny, Doris. We had things like smart-asses way back then, too," Dot's mother said, cocking an eyebrow. "I'll have you know, that ornament is very rare."

Aunt Doris sniffed, then rummaged around in the box. "Ah ha! Here he is! In all his glory, wearing his purple and black jumpsuit. I like these new glass ornaments you see everywhere. You can certainly carry out a theme more easily these days. I love themed trees, don't you? I saw some cute coyote ornaments down at the WallyMart the other day. I guess those would be for a Southwestern theme tree. I even saw some severed monkey head ornaments. Now that's bizarre."

Dot shuddered.

"Really?" Dot's mother asked, distracted. "That's interesting. I wonder if I could find some more Elvis ornaments? Perhaps we could do an all Elvis tree. We could fill in with little tiny vinyl records. They'd be black, so that would work with the color scheme."

"No way, Nancy Lee! Remember? All modern? We voted on it back in October. Plain balls. No figurative ornaments. Period. We do not want to divert from that, because it would look all disjointed and out of whack. And very un-theme-like. I'm just letting you put ONE Elvis on there because I know you'll throw a wall-eyed fit if you don't get your way. And I wish you'd hide him in the back."

Dot poked around in the ornament box and pulled out a moth-eaten flocked Santa ornament. "Oh look at this! I remember it from when I was a kid. I love these vintage decorations! Can we put it up somewhere?"

"Nope," Aunt Doris said. "No figuratives. Except for your mother's Elvis, that is."

Dot frowned and put the ornament back in the box. "I guess Santa is out this year then. What's in this?" Dot indicated an old ragged cardboard box that sat underneath the ornaments. She pulled on the top flap and a cloud of dust flew up in her face.

"Ooof!" Dot sat back and stared. "Look at all of this stuff! What is it?"

Her mother shrugged. "Oh, it's just some old toys of yours I found up in the attic. They were stored with the decorations. I was going to pitch them out. They're so dirty! I should have thrown them out years ago."

Dot dug through the box, pulling out a wad of black fabric. She turned it over in her hands for a few seconds. "Oh look! Here's my little stuffed cat I made out of an old black sock. He's got green button eyes. I named him 'Cattywampus.' Do you remember?" she asked, digging further into the box. She pulled out another object. It was an old rag doll with sewn-on clothes and two tiny buttons for eyes. She had crude stubs for arms and legs and her misshapen feet were stuffed into a tiny pair of plastic boots. "And Bo Raggley!" she squealed hugging the doll to her breast. "I made these when I was about ten-years old. They were some of my first sewing projects. I loved this doll! I tried cramming some of my Barbie boots on her, but they didn't exactly fit."

"Yes, I can see that," her mother said, nodding. "I remember when you made those, and we had to cart you to the emergency room when you poked the sewing machine needle through your fingernail. Your daddy was quite put out with you when he discovered you'd been into his sock drawer looking for materials."

Dot laughed as she continued to dig through the box. "And look…here's Steven's little metal robot! It's all rusted now," she said, sadly.

"Your brother never did keep his toys nice, like you did," Aunt Doris said. "He took it apart a few times, put it back together then abandoned it for something newer and left it to rust out in the back garden. I'm surprised it's still in one piece."

"They aren't nice anymore." Dot's mother picked up the doll and held her nose. "Eww, she's a mess—looks like the silverfish made a nest in her hair."

Aunt Doris took the stuffed creature from Dot. "Stuffed cat? Are you sure this a cat? Hmmm, I sort of see the resemblance. Ah, yes, here's a tail. UNstuffed cat is more like it. He looks like he needs a few stitches here and there."

"Or a trip to the trash bin," her mother sniffed.

Dot snatched the stuffed toy away from her aunt. "Don't make fun of my creations! I thought these were gone a long time ago."

"Now I'm in a big de-cluttering frenzy and it's time to get rid of some of this old stuff," her mother said. "All of my friends are doing it, and I don't want to get left behind. If you want those, you'll have to take them home with you."

Dot nodded and continued to dig through the box. "Oh, look! Here's grandma's old manger scene." She carefully removed a rickety cardboard stable and a few small figures.

Her aunt smiled. "The fancy folks around here call it a créche, Dot. It has more of an international connotation that way."

"I don't care what they call it now. I love these little rubber sheep and the camels. They don't make things the same anymore. Now they're all plastic or resin. And look at these little chalkware angels! They still have the prices written in pencil on the bottom! Fifteen-cents each!" Dot said, in amazement.

Her mother smiled. "We bought those at the Woolworth's downtown before it closed. You used to play with all those when you were little. I remember you just about swallowed Baby Jesus one year and we had to turn you upside down to get Him to come back out."

Dot looked horrified. "I did not!"

Her aunt laughed. "Oh, yes you did. Don't you see the teeth marks? There on the side?"

Dot took a closer look then winced. Sure enough, baby Jesus had been chomped. "I don't remember that," she said, then continued to dig through the box. "Oh, look! You kept my little Christmas fairy!"

"Yes," her mother said. "I did keep it. Unfortunately."

Dot smiled. "We had an argument about whether it was appropriate to use a fairy on a Texas Christmas tree. I read a book in school about the British tradition of using fairies instead of angels and I was determined to have one. You finally gave in and we sat up all night making her. Remember that?"

Doris nodded. "I do! I also remember that you threw a big ol' hissy fit because we didn't have anything fancy for her skirt and I had to sacrifice one of my old net petticoats for her dress. And we had to make an emergency run to the dime store to buy glitter. That was a fun time. Why don't we make things now like we used to?"

Dot's mother wrinkled her nose. "Too messy."

Dot wished that Christmas could be fun again. Too bad people had to grow up and put all the fun behind them. She gazed at her mother. "Can't we put her at the top of the tree? Please, mama?"

Her mother shook her head. "Sorry, Dot. I already bought a purple pointy light-up thing for the top. It was very expensive. AND it matches the balls."

Dot picked up the rubber sheep and the chalkware angel. "Can we at least put these out someplace?" She glanced around the room. The mantle was packed with crystal candlesticks and clear glass decanters filled with purple sparkly things. She frowned. The coffee table was covered with a huge centerpiece made of purple glittered pinecones.

"I don't know, Dot," her mother said reluctantly. "I just don't see where we'd put it. We really didn't plan on displaying it this year."

Doris took the chalkware angel from Dot. "Here, let me have it. I'll find a place for these. After all, the set was your grandmother's. We probably should make an effort. Maybe I can sit it on the shelf in the bathroom above the toilet. Or in the kitchen. Wouldn't it be nice in the kitchen? We could see baby Jesus first thing in the morning when we go in for coffee."

Dot began to gather up the toys. "Thanks, Aunt Doris. I think I'll take these up to my room. I'll decide what to do with them later. Maybe I can repair this stuffed cat. Do you have a needle and thread here somewhere?"

Her mother shrugged. "If I do, I don't know where they'd be. I haven't sewn anything by hand in years. Anyway, I think that old thing needs to be pitched out in the trash. Remember your dust mite allergies, dear! And your asthma. Those old toys must be packed with dust mites by now! Ugh, filthy things!"

"Oh, I'll be fine, mother. Stop fussing over me. I'm thirty-two-years old. I'm not a little kid anymore," Dot said, sneezing.

"Well, honestly, sometimes I do wonder," her mother said, handing her a tissue. "You live in a dream world, Dot. You always were the dreamer in the family. I thought that would change as you got older. You need to come into the real world. Wake up and smell the French roast coffee beans!"

"I'm not sure I want to live in the real world," Dot admitted. "Especially if it involves French roast beans! Sometimes it seems like it's all just a little bit too real for me."

She yawned, and her mother pulled her into an embrace. "You're tired; get some sleep. Good night, sweetie."

Her aunt smiled and said, "Sweet dreams, little girl."

Dot took one last look around the livingroom, kissed them both good night, sneezed again, and wearily climbed upstairs to her old bedroom.

She flipped on the light and smiled at the twin bed and smoothed the old chenille bedspread covering the top. Having the old things around was comforting. She lined the toys up on the top of the old bookshelf, quickly undressed for bed, pulled back the covers, and climbed in for a few moments. She finally got back up, grabbed the stuffed cat and pulled it into bed with her. She put it beside her pillow, sneezed then turned over. The last thing Dot remembered was the toy cat falling over, nudging the side of her head. She pushed it away and fell into a deep sleep.

CHAPTER TWO

Some time later, Dot awoke to some very bright lights. At first, she thought they were emergency flashers. She squinted, sat up and realized she was no longer in her bed. She was outside, in a very strange place. Colors of bright royal blue, red, green, silver and sparkly-white shone everywhere. Traditional Christmas colors. Winter wonderland colors. Very bright colors—so bright they hurt her eyes. A very cold wind was blowing and her nose stung. She shook her head, trying to clear her vision. Where was she?

Dot looked around and her eyes almost popped out of her head. She saw giant lollypops—like ancient trees—standing beside the road. Huge boxes gaily wrapped in figured paper with bright red bows perched on top were piled under them. Giant candy canes sprouted up like telephone poles and went as far as Dot could see. An odd green and red path snaked through a forest of candy. It seemed to be paved with sugar.

Way off in the distance, Dot saw some murky pointy buildings of some sort—almost like castles. "Oh dear," she said. "I don't think I'm in Texas anymore!"

Dot rubbed her eyes, turned over and found herself entwined with a very large black cat—almost as large as she was. Just then, the cat also woke up, started squirming and struggling to get untangled.

"Let go of me!" he hissed. "You're squishing too hard! Quit squeezing me! You're smothering me! Ffft! Ffft!"

The cat hissed and spit and struggled until he was finally free. He jumped to his feet, arched his back, spit again, shook, stretched and clenched his back. Then he yawned with his huge mouth wide open, showing a large set of pointy teeth.

Dot stared. "What the . . .?" she stuttered, then jumped up, whirled around, staring at the scenery. She looked down and realized she was wearing an elf costume.

"Where the heck am I? And where on earth did I get these clothes?" she asked. "No wonder I'm freezing!" She tugged at the short skirt.

The cat shrugged as he continued to stretch. "Don't ask me! But I will say you look absolutely adorable in that skirt!"

Dot glared.

"For what it's worth," the cat said, "I'm not sure we ARE on earth! I just woke up and imagine my surprise to find myself wrapped in the arms of a HUMAN BEING," he said, shuddering. "Imagine my disgust. I feel like I've been cramped up in a cage for thousands of years! Nay, millions of years!" He glanced at her. "Although, you are kinda cute."

Dot stared at the cat then poked him. "Oh. My. You're . . . real. And you seem to have gotten larger. And you talk."

The cat hissed. "What are you trying to imply, that I've gained weight? How dare you!" He turned his back to her and started grooming, licking his paws and admiring himself. He plopped down, hiked his back leg, then froze and stared. "Do you mind?"

Dot whirled around with her back to him. "Sorry. No, I didn't mean…well, never mind. I don't know what I meant. I just woke up. Or at least, I think I did. I'm not so sure. I may be dreaming."

The cat nodded. "We may both be dreaming. Although I very seldom dream of humans."

Dot decided to ignore that remark. "Would you look at this place! It's a wonderland. It's so pretty! It's so colorful! Look at all the giant candy!" Dot said.

"And look at all the pressies!" the cat said, running around, checking the names on the tags. "Oh bugger," he muttered. "I don't see any for me. Well, there's still time. We have days before Christmas—plenty of time for more shopping." He sighed. "Christmas! All that wonderful paper to jump in, and all those lovely empty boxes. I do so LOVE Christmas!

Dot stared at him. "So do I!"

"It's such a wonderful time of the year!" he sang. "It's a time for WANTING. A time to tell everybody what I WANT, a time to BEG people for what I WANT and demand that they get it for ME. And if they don't get ME what I WANT, well then, I'LL have to make life very difficult for them! No matter what! Because what I WANT is what I must HAVE! Woohoo!" He smoothed the fur on his chest. "Pardon me; sometimes I get carried away when thinking about the holiday festivities."

Dot stared at the cat. "I'm not so much into the wanting thing. I'm pretty satisfied with what I have."

The cat shrugged and flexed his claws. "I am a cat. Wanting is what I do. *Wanting* would be my middle name, if I didn't already have one."

"You have a name?" Dot asked.

"Yes, I do, as a matter of fact!" the cat exclaimed, bowing. "Cattywampus Bonaparte is my name. Extreme pleasure is my game!"

Dot groaned. "I was afraid of that."

"But you can call me King Bonaparte, if you wish," he added.

Suddenly, a metallic whirring noise sounded from behind one of the wrapped gifts. A toy robot rolled out, clicking and clacking and grinding gears. It stopped, and smoke puffed from its head.

"I am Mod-el Num-ber Five Four Nine Sev-en dash Three. Also known as Ro-bot. I have been pro-grammed to pro-vide ass-is-tance. Would you like to play? Would you like to play? There is noth-ing that you need?" The robot clanked and knocked.

The cat hissed, bushed his tail then jumped back behind Dot. "Ay chi-hua-hua mama! This rusty bucket of bolts can TALK!"

Dot stared at the robot, then the cat. "Why do you find that so strange? You're talking, too!"

The robot whirred. "Yes. I do par-tic-i-pate in hu-man speech. I have lim-i-ted a-bil-i-ty to speak. And on-ly in ro-bot-ic mon-o-tones. Sad to say."

A small, soft voice called out from behind one of the boxes. "Could someone please help me outta here? I'm having a very hard time with these damned boots for some reason."

A raggedy old doll crawled out from behind the box. She was dressed in a tattered calico dress, dotted bloomers and very small cowboy boots. Dot rushed over and helped her stand.

The doll smoothed her dress. "Thank you kindly. Hello. My name is Bo Raggley. What's yours?" the doll asked. "Would you like to have a tea party?"

Cattywampus jumped back, hissing.

"My name is Dot. Dorothy Norton. And I . . .wait a minute, what am I doing, answering a doll! You're all talking? Where am I? Is this a dream? If so, I want to wake up! Like, NOW!" Dot jumped up and down and started slapping her own face. "Wake up, wake up, wake up!" she yelled. "Crap! This usually works. I don't know why this isn't working."

The cat nodded. "See! There is something you want! Here, let me try. This is one of my spec-i-al-it-ies! This is what cats do. We are masters at waking people up." He grabbed her hair and tugged, peered into her face, waggled his tail in her nose and stuck it into her ears. He meowed loudly and put his two huge front paws on her shoulders and kneaded her like bread dough.

"Rawwwrhhh, meeeeeow, meeeowwww, rawwwrhhhh," Cattywampus caterwauled. "Wake up, get up, I need food, I need to go ouuuut! Rawwwrhhhh."

Dot struggled out of his clutches. "What in the hell! Never mind. Geez, get off me."

"You are a strange human being, Dorothy Norton," the cat said.

"I'm strange?" she asked.

"You cannot make me believe that you do not want things," the cat said. "Every human being wants something."

Dot thought about it for a minute. "Well, sure, I want things I can't have. I want world peace, an end to world hunger, more government subsidies for small farms…that sort of thing."

Bo Raggley nodded, her head flopping back and forth. "We all want those things."

The cat waggled his head. "No, we don't, Sawdust Girl! And as for you, Dot, I've heard all that before. Blah blah blah. Are you sure you don't want STUFF? I'll bet you want a new car!"

She shrugged. "Not so much. The old one I have is perfectly fine," Dot said. "And it gets good mileage. It's only got 124,000 miles on it."

"Wow. Are you really a human being? Because I'm getting a bit incredulous here," Cattywampus said, tapping his foot. "Very incredulous, in fact. A real human being would love a new car. So therefore, you are not real."

"Of course I'm a real human being!" Dot said. "Now that's just absurd."

"I wish I was a real human being," Bo Raggley whined. "I really WANT to be a human being. Then I could wear different clothes everyday. Do you know how boring it is to wear the same outfit day after day after day after year after year after year after…"

The cat waved her away. "Geez! OK! We get the picture! Personally, I think you're much better off as a doll. I would think being a doll would be infinitely preferable. You wouldn't have to do common labour, people would do things for you and carry you around where you want to go. Perhaps they'd even put you in a little carriage and take you out into the sunshine and have elegant tea parties with little bone china cups and cake!"

"Hmmm, you do have a point there," Bo said.

"That's why I want to be a REAL CAT!"

"So you can have tea parties?" Bo Raggley asked, sweetly.

Cattywampus shook his head. "No! Of course not! So people will do all sorts of things for me! They'll put me in a little basket and carry me around, and they'll buy emerald-studded collars for me and feed me fancy foods on crystal dishes! I saw it all on television!"

Bo Raggley frowned at him. "That sounds quite selfish of you."

"And your point is? Hey, look at me. I'm a cat. It's something else I do well," he answered. "Besides, that's very rich of you, coming from a rag doll."

"Rag doll?" she whimpered. "I'm not a rag doll. Am I?"

"Guys!" Dot yelled. "Actually, there is something I want. I want you all to be quiet so I can think." She looked around. "I want to know where we are, and how we got here."

"That certainly would be nice to know," the cat admitted.

Dot pulled a cell phone out of a tiny pocket in her skirt. "I wonder…Dang! No signal."

Cattywampus stared at the phone. "What good is that thing? Can it triangulate our whereabouts, pinpointing our location so we can be tracked by the authorities? Does it send out a homing beacon notifying your parents where you are? Phones on TV do all that stuff."

"Afraid not," Dot said. "This phone isn't a smart phone. It's a stupid phone."

"No GPS cap-a-bil-ities?" Robot asked.

"Nope, no GPS either."

"Then what GOOD is it?" the cat asked. "Might as well use it for a paperweight."

"I can get calls on it. And I can call people back. If it's charged properly." Dot stared at the phone. "But I always forget to do that."

"Oh niiiice!" Bo said, plopping down on the ground.

"But look on the bright side," Dot said. "Wherever we are, this place is gorgeous! It's just like one of those vintage Christmas cards. It's like an old-fashioned Christmas! And, come to think of it, there IS something I want. I want an old-fashioned Christmas. A Christmas with handmade cat toys made out of old socks with button eyes and stuffed dolls made from sewing scraps and little bits of rick-rack and metal robots and trucks for little boys to play with. I want a Christmas where people don't decorate their trees with purple and black Elvis ornaments!" She took a breath. "What does Elvis have to do with Christmas, anyway?" She plopped down on the ground next to Bo and wiped a tear from her eye.

Cattywampus frowned. "Didn't Elvis do some Christmas albums? They advertise them on TV, right? I seem to remember some. There was that really cool song he sang." The cat struck a pose then began to howl. "I'll have a blue hoo-hoo Christmas without youuuuu, hoo, hoo, hoo!" He gyrated a bit then bowed.

"Wow. You cannot sing," Dot sniffed. "Not even one little bit."

Robot whirred and twirled. "Af-firm-a-tive. And you can-not dance."

Dot helped Bo up off the ground. "Never mind the singing OR the dancing. This is not the time to feel sorry for ourselves. Don't worry; something's bound to happen. Surely somebody knows where we are!"

All of a sudden, there was a loud CRASH and something clattered down from the sky. It was a young woman, and she was dressed in a 1950-style party dress with a frothy pink skirt. She had tiny pink transparent wings. It was a Christmas fairy! A pair of pointy cat's eye glasses with rhinestones perched on her nose and her hair was upswept into a beehive hairdo—a very high, purple sparkled beehive.

She bopped the cat on the nose with her magic wand. "First of all, stop that bloody howling this instant! No singing of copyrighted songs!" she warbled in a very British accent. "Have you gone totally mental?"

The cat rubbed his head. "Oww, that hurt! And who are you to tell me that I can't sing?"

"Isn't it obvious?" she said, doing a little pirouette and waving her wand around. "I'm the freakin' Christmas Fairy, and I'm here to keep you out of trouble, to fulfill your wishes and give you what you want. Well, not really. I'm mostly here to tell you where to go. Not really. Oh buggeration! I'm not doing this right. I'm so out of practice. Let me start again. I'm here to give you some guidance. Right, that's better! And I'm here to tell you that there's only one person who can fulfill all your wishes!"

"And who's that?" Cattywampus asked.

"The Giver of All Good Things, the Maestro of Mistletoe, the Grand Hoo-Hah of Holidays . . . Jolly old Saint Nick himself!" the fairy said, waving her wand all around, higgledy-piggledy.

"Santa Clause?" they all asked, in harmony.

The fairy nodded. "Yes! The one, the only, the REAL Santa Clause! He can do anything."

"Anything?" Bo asked. "Wow!"

The fairy frowned. "Well, almost anything. It's possible there are a few things he can't do."

"Pffftz!" Cattywampus spit. "I don't believe in Santa Clause. There's no such thing as Santa Clause. He's one of those myths made up by humans, right? To keep bad little children from doing stupid things like pulling cat tails? Right?"

Bo Raggley smiled a sweet little rag doll smile. "I've always wanted to believe Santa

Clause was real. It would be nice to think that I was born at the North Pole then dropped down a chimney on Christmas Eve into the loving arms of a real little girl. Isn't that how all of you were born?" She gazed at Dot. "Isn't that how I came to live with you?"

Dot didn't have the heart to tell her how she'd really been born—like a tiny little Frankenstein's monster, made up of scraps and rags and stuffed with sawdust from the floor of her father's workshop.

The cat slapped his thighs and doubled over with laughter. "Ahahahahaha! That's funny! Face it, Patchwork Girl, you came out of somebody's rag bag. You're made up of scraps and a bit of stuffing!"

The doll sobbed. "I don't believe you! You're such a horrid old thing!"

Dot decided not to mention how the cat had started out.

The fairy flitted back and forth. "Technically, there is a real Santa Clause. But he's in a transition state right now and is, well, having a slight difficulty. He's going through a bad patch. Your timing definitely sucks, but never mind that. If anyone can help you, he can! You must go see him," she ordered. "Right away."

"Why?" Dot asked. "Why the rush?"

The fairy shrugged. "Otherwise, we don't have much of a story, do we?" she answered. "And I would have wasted all this time when I could be sitting at the pub instead drinking a nice pint of ale and chattin' up the blokes."

"I just want to go home!" Dot said. "Or to wake up! Or something! This is all crazy! It's just a dream, right? Please tell me it's a dream."

The fairy shook her head. "I can't really say. What is a dream? Is life reality, or a wakeful dream? Sorry, now that we've started this journey, you cannot wake up, if you are indeed asleep, until you've traveled down the road and visited the real Santa Clause and told him your wishes!"

Dot stared at the fairy. "Are you friggin' kidding me?"

The fairy bopped Dot on the head with her wand. "Tsk tsk, watch your bloody language!" she said. "To answer your probably rhetorical question—it was rhetorical, wasn't it? Nope, sorry. No kidding allowed. This is totally serious business."

The robot screeched up with a clash of gears and a lot of clicking. "How do we find San-ta Clause? Please e-lab-o-rate and I will set de-sired co-or-din-ates and nav-i-gate to the place of his res-i-dence."

The cat whooped. "Hey, who needs GPS when we have this guy!"

The fairy smiled. "Oh, it's a lot easier than that. All you have to do is snap your fingers three times, and say 'Follow the Rudolph the Red-Nosed Reindeer Road.' Say it over and over. That will lead you to the North Pole. Well, not actually the North Pole. Santa had to move the Pole farther south a few years ago. But still, it's in the same general direction. Climate change, you know. Things melting all over the place." The fairy shivered. "Bad bit of business, that."

Dot frowned, wringing her hands. "Oh dear! I do so worry about that! Don't you?"

"Yes, well, we're all concerned. Santa's working on that one," the Christmas fairy admitted. "Give him time!"

"All right, then," Dot said, snapping her fingers. "Follow the Rudolph the Red-Nosed Reindeer Road. Boy, that's a mouthful, isn't it? Follow…that sounds so familiar! Now WHY does that sound so familiar to me?"

"I don't have fingers! How am I supposed to snap? This is just not convenient," Cattywampus said. "Not convenient at all. Isn't there something else we could do?"

Bo Raggley started crying. "Me neither! I just have stumps for hands! How am I supposed to snap my fingers if all I have is stumps?" she sobbed.

The robot whirred. "I do not have dig-its like hu-man be-ings. This does not com-pute. This does not com-pute. Warn-ing warn-ing!" Robot flung his arms around.

The fairy folded her arms and frowned. "Well, bollocks! Very well! Forget the snapping! I just thought you might want to build up some rhythm to get you on your way. Some motivation, some impetus, a little bit of jazz! Just say 'Follow the Jingle Bell Jaunt!' etcetera, etcetera then."

"Wait, you changed it!" Cattywampus said. "I thought you said to follow the Rudolph the Red-Nosed Reindeer Road?"

"I did?" the fairy asked. "Hmmm, I'm sure I said to follow the Kris Kringle Highway. Didn't I? Are you sure?"

"Warn-ing! Warn-ing! This does not compute!" Robot wheezed.

The fairy shrugged. "Oh, for crying out loud! Just follow the bloomin' road, will ya? You're liable to get somewhere, eventually. I can't stand around in the cold all day playing at silly buggers with you lot." She turned to leave.

"Wait! Do you have any other advice for us?" Dot asked.

The Christmas fairy shook her head. "No, not really. That should do it. Be on your way, then." She turned to leave, then stopped. "Wait! Yes! I forgot! There is one other tiny thing. Beware of the insanely ravenous invisible flying monkeys!"

"There's no such thing as invisible flying monkeys! I know those are a myth!" Cattywampus retorted. "You're just trying to scare us."

"Weren't there some sort of flying monkeys in the Wiz . . ." Dot started. Before she could finish the sentence, there was the most awful racket like thousands of wings flapping, squawking, and screeching. The fairy shrieked and poofed away in a cloud of glittery sparkle. The air filled with the sound of a thousand flying monkeys. Except, of course, they were invisible. Just like the fairy warned. And most likely ravenous, too.

The robot turned around in a circle, flinging his arms up and down. "Warn-ing, warn-ing. Must run. Now."

Cattywampus ducked, swatting at the invisible monkeys. "Quick, Robot! Shoot them with a ray gun, or ex-ter-min-ate them, or something, for pete's sake!"

"I do not un-der-stand," the robot said.

"Can't you kill them?" the cat asked, swatting.

The robot's gears ground for a moment. "Neg-a-tory good bud-dy. I am Mod-el Num-ber Five Four Nine Sev-en dash Three. I do not have ca-pa-bil-i-ties for shoo-ting."

"Oh great!" Cattywampus said then ducked, pulling Dot and Bo behind one of the giant candy canes. "Now you tell us!"

CHAPTER THREE

The next morning, the small group cautiously crept out of their hiding place and was glad to see that the invisible flying monkeys had dispersed. As far as they could tell, anyway. At any rate, they didn't hear any squawking and shrieking. They wandered up one lane of the windy, snaky road to another. After chanting "Follow the Rudolph the Red-Nosed Reindeer Road" and "Follow the Jingle Bell Jaunt" and "Follow the Kris Kringle Highway" for several hours, until they were sick to death of it, they were knackered. And very grumpy.

"We must have been walking for hours!" Dot said. "I'm not even sure we're making any progress."

"Shew!" the cat said. "At least we got away from those flying banana breaths."

"Don't forget the invisible ravenous part," Bo said, shivering.

"That was odd, wasn't it?" Dot asked.

"We have been walking forever! These boots are not made for walkin'. I need to rest. Can we stop for a minute, please?" Bo asked and plopped down on the ground.

The robot whirred and clicked. "I wish I was not so rus-ty. My ret-ro rock-ets could move us a-bout much fast-er."

Dot frowned. "I have a bad feeling about this whole thing. This is bound to be dangerous. I'm not sure we should follow that strange fairy's advice. I keep expecting something to jump out from behind these candy canes."

Cattywampus snorted. "Yeah? Like what? A green witch, perhaps?"

Dot frowned and looked over her shoulder. "Maybe. It could happen. It happens in Broadway plays, in movies and on TV. Why not here?"

"Wouldn't that be deliciously *wicked* fun?" Cattywampus whooped. "I'd tear her from limb to limb!" he said, clawing the air. "I'd scratch her eyes out!"

"What do we do now?" Bo whined.

Cattywampus frowned and made a rude noise. "You want to get back home, don't you? What a buncha scaredy cats! The Christmas Fairy said that we couldn't go back until we find Santa Clause and tell him what we want. Right?" the cat asked.

Dot nodded. "Right."

"So, that's what we have to do! Are you going to chicken out now? We've come so far! At least fifty-feet. What are you, cowardly?"

Bo frowned. "Of course she isn't cowardly! Dot's going to lead us down the road and help us get what we want. She's very brave! Isn't that right, Dot?"

Dot shrugged. "What gave you that idea? This is not just a walk in the park, you know. It's a danger-filled, high stakes gamble, very risky. VERY risky. I'm not sure I'm up to it, to tell the truth."

"You are too brave!" Bo said. "My whole life, I've only wanted to be brave like you.

Remember when you were a little girl, and that mean dog came into the back yard and grabbed me and pulled me into the garden and started throwing me back and forth? I thought he'd shake my stuffing out! And remember when that same dog tried to bury me, like a dried up old bone?"

"That figures! The cad! Dogs can be such Neanderthals sometimes," Cattywampus sniffed. "The brutes!"

Dot shook her head. "I...uh...I'm sorry, doesn't ring a bell."

"And remember when we were having a tea party, and that snooty Annabelle Mc-What's-Her-Face said I looked like an old pile of dirty snot rags?" Bo continued. "And you pushed her over into a puddle? And snatched a wad of her hair out?"

Dot frowned. "I don't quite remember that, either. That was a long time ago, Bo."

"And then there was that time when your mother had to sew my arm back on after I accidentally got underneath the lawn mower, and you held me like I was a real baby and told me not to cry?" Bo said, exasperated.

Dot nodded. "Yes! I actually DO remember that! Your parts were all over the yard! I had to . . . uh, never mind."

"Ever since then, I've believed you were the bravest human I've ever known. And I wanted to be just like you. You always wear such cool clothes, too. Removable ones. I know you can get us back home," Bo said.

39

Dot squirmed. "Oh crap. All right. I'll do it. How could I leave you behind now?"

The robot pulled up beside Dot and whirred. "Par-don me for in-ter-rup-ting your nos-tal-gic in-ter-lude. It has come to my at-ten-tion that we might be walk-ing in a cir-cul-ar pat-tern."

"No, that's not right! We can't be!" Dot said, pointing off into the distance. "Look! Up ahead! A castle!"

"That's it! It's Santa's Workshop! We made it. It IS real!" Cattywampus howled and danced a little jig. "What are we waiting for? Exit, stage left!"

CHAPTER FOUR

It seemed to Dot like they walked for days after spotting the building, but eventually they made it to their destination. Sure enough, right outside the door there was a large sign that read "Santa's Workshop." The outside of the building was made out of something that looked like sugar and it sparkled in the sunlight. A large wooden door was carved with tiny reindeer and looked very old and there was a huge wrought-iron doorknocker shaped like a snowflake.

"I'll bet it's beautiful inside," Bo said, her eyes twinkling.

Well, they would have been if buttons could twinkle.

"I'll bet it smells wonderful, too," she continued, "all piney and sugary and Christmasy inside."

Cattywampus snorted. "Where on earth do you get these ideas?" the cat asked, rolling his eyes.

"Oh, leave her alone," Dot said. "Be nice. After all, she might be right." She shivered and tugged at her skirt. "I just hope it's warmer inside."

"We shall see for ourselves," Cattywampus said as he picked up the huge knocker and banged it against the door.

A robotic voice encouraged him to enter a code into the keypad beside the door.

"What the...?" Cattywampus said. "We don't have a code. That blasted fairy didn't tell us anything about a code."

Robot whirred a bit, rolled up to the keypad and buzzed and binged. A green laser-like light scanned the pad. "It seems to be some high-tech giz-mo. I can-not ac-cess it."

"Oh, for pete's sake," Dot said. "Let me handle this." She banged on the door again. "Please, let us in. We're freezing! We weren't given any kind of code when we were told to come here. "

"And starving," Cattywampus added. "I could certainly eat." He turned to Dot. "Could you eat? Aren't you hungry, too?"

Just then a tiny door in the middle of the large door opened with a squeak. A booming voice asked "Who's there? Go away."

Dot glanced at Cattywampus. "Dorothy Norton and friends. We're here to see Santa Clause."

"Don't know anybody named Santa Clause. Perhaps you have the wrong house."

"Are you kiddin' me? This is the right house. It's the ONLY house out here," the cat said.

"Who told you to come here?" the voice asked.

"The Christmas fairy," Bo said.

"No such thing! Go away," the voice said.

Just then a small herd of reindeer ambled by, pawing and nibbling at the snow.

Cattywampus pushed Bo aside. "Look here—there's lots of snow, crystals, sparkles, glitter out the wazoo and a herd of reindeer meandering around out front. I'm pretty sure we're in the right place. Now open up!"

"Not to mention the sign that says Santa's Workshop," Bo whispered.

A little brown face popped into the window. He wore a little pointy hat and a frown and Dot was pretty sure he was an elf. "We ain't got no steenkin' reindeer," he said. "You're mistaken. Like I mentioned. Go. Away."

"What are those four-leggeds then?" Cattywampus asked. "If not reindeer?"

"Those are watchdogs," the elf said. "Ferocious big watchdogs with very pointy teeth. They are very dangerous creatures. To keep intruders away."

"With antlers?" Dot asked. "Now I've heard everything!"

"Cheeky monkeys, ain't you?" the elf asked. "I'm under orders. Nobody gets in. We're not open to the public. Don't make me come out there and…"

A soft female voice interrupted. "Herman, who's at the door?"

The face disappeared, some grumblings were heard and the door opened. A short female elf stepped out and smiled at Dot. "Don't mind Herman. He takes his role entirely too seriously. Now, what can I help you with? Oh my goodness, my manners are atrocious! Come in! Come in out of the cold."

Dot, Cattywampus, Robot and Bo slowly walked through the door.

"Please wait here," the elf said. "Someone will be with you shortly." All of a sudden, she disappeared, leaving them standing in a small entryway at the end of a hallway. Christmas carols were playing over a tinny loudspeaker. It was chilly in the room and Dot shivered. The group waited for a few moments and the cat paced.

"Geez, are we gonna have to stand around all day?" Cattywampus wondered. "Because I'm ready to get this show on the road."

Dot nodded and motioned for the small group to proceed. They cautiously walked down the hallway. At the end, there was one door. She shrugged, turned the doorknob, opened the door and they shuffled inside.

The room was large, white, and sterile, and reminded Dot of a scientific laboratory. Around the corner there were huge stacks of plain brown boxes, all stamped on the side with the words "MADE ON MARS." Along the back wall, a huge bank of computers whirred, beeped and calculated.

"Wow," Bo whispered. "Talk about great expectations, dashed to bits."

"THIS is Santa's Workshop? I don't believe it," Dot said.

Cattywampus pointed. "Look!"

A polished wooden desk the size of a king-sized bed sat in the middle of the room. A large man dressed in red velvet and fur hunched over the desk, shuffling through reams of paper reports and old computer printouts. From time to time, he turned to the side and pounded on an old keyboard, stared into an ancient monitor and grumbled to himself. He wadded the papers into balls and threw them in the general direction of a large wastepaper basket the size of a Buick. It was overflowing and the floor was littered with the debris.

Dot sucked in a breath. Santa Clause!

The place was chaotic with clanging, banging and clacking noises and an old black telephone sat on the edge of the desk, ringing insistently.

Finally, Santa stopped to answer the phone.

"Speak! What? More delays?" he barked. "A meteor shower? Damn! That's all we need right now! What next? Yes . . . No. No! I specifically said four thousand of those. Right. All in a neutral color. All the same size. No, not blue. Yes, that's right—beige! Beige, I said! We'll save money if they're all beige. I am the great Santa Clause! I have spoken!" He slammed the receiver down. "Buncha idjits!" he muttered.

Dot glanced at her companions then inched forward. "Excuse me, sir."

"What? Who are you? How did you get in here? Go away!" Santa shouted. "I'm busy. I don't have time for visitors now! Who dares to disturb me? I am the great Santa Clause!"

The visitors cautiously inched closer to the desk.

"Wow, would you look at this place?" the cat whispered. "Where are all the elves? I thought there would be lots of elves!" he said.

Santa looked up and frowned. "What do YOU want? How did you get in here? Herman! Guards!"

"Wait!" Bo shouted and blushed. "Please hear us out."

Santa squinted at her and blew out a breath. "Well, then. Aren't you a fine mess? All right then, but hurry up; I don't have all day. Speak!" Santa ordered. "Or I'll have your heads chopped off! Don't see if I won't!"

Dot and Cattywampus cowered in fear and Bo started sobbing. Again.

Santa smiled an evil little smile. "Oh, go dry up, I wouldn't really do that. But I like saying it anyway. It helps blow off some of this negative energy. It's hell being freakin' Santa all the time."

Finally, the robot rolled forward, his gears whirring. "Gree-tings, earth-ling. We come in peace."

"What's the meaning of this?" Santa shouted. "A human in a skimpy outfit, a rag doll, an overgrown cat and a rusty old robot? Why are you here? Once again, who are you? How did you get in? You're wasting my valuable time! Get to the point."

"I wish people would quit calling me a rag doll," Bo whispered.

Cattywampus pushed the robot aside. "Oh for pete's sake! Let me do the talkin'. You've seen too many bad sci-fi movies, Robot." He turned to Santa. "My esteemed sir!" he said, bowing. "Allow me to introduce myself! My name is Cattywampus Horatio Bonaparte, at your service, sir."

"Horatio?" Dot asked. "Really?"

Dot and Bo looked at each other and shrugged.

"And who are the rest of you?" Santa asked.

"My name is Bo Raggley. I'm a doll," Bo said, and curtsied.

"Somewhat obvious," Santa sniffed. He stared at Dot. "And you are?"

"My name is Dot…Dorothy Norton. My friends call me Dot. I'm a human being. Obviously. I'm not exactly sure why we're here. The Christmas Fairy sent us here and I'd really like to…"

"Not that blasted fairy story again!" Santa said, interrupting her. "Egads. I really wish whoever is pretending to be that Christmas fairy would quit sending people up here to bother me. She doesn't know her bum from a hole in the ground! Always sending people off on the Reindeer Road, or the Jingle Way or some such nonsense. She's nuttier than a fruitcake!"

"Next!" Santa shouted, gesturing at the robot.

The robot rolled forward. "And I am Model Number Five Four Nine Sev-en dash Three."

Cattywampus stepped forward. "Now that we've all been introduced. Let me just say, kind sir, we have traveled for hours, fighting off horrible invisible ravenous flying monkeys, facing starvation and the threat of certain death from unknown creatures. We have been in fear for our lives, what with the possibility of green witches leaping out from behind rocks and such. All this just to meet you, and to beseech your favors," he simpered. He took a deep breath then bowed. "We are your humble subjects."

"Oh, brother," Bo Raggley whispered.

The robot whirred and said, "It is get-ting deep in here."

Santa frowned. "Green witches? Tell me, did you actually ever run across any green witches?"

"Well, no," Dot admitted. "We didn't actually see any. But just because we didn't, that doesn't mean they aren't real."

"I did mention the *possibility* of green witches, did I not?" Cattywampus said. "You see, we could have run into all sorts of horrible things out there. One never knows."

"What a bunch of rubbish! Just as I suspected. There are no green witches!" Santa bellowed. "And there's no such thing as the Christmas Fairy, either! If there was such a person, I'd certainly know about it. Why are you really here? Are you spies, perhaps?" Santa bellowed, suspicious. "Who really sent you?"

"No, we aren't spies!" the cat said. "And the Christmas Fairy DID send us here. We only want to ask of you a few small favors. You see, there are things that each of us want, and . . ."

"Silence! What? WANT?" Santa screamed, pounding on his desk. "Somebody else who WANTS something? I KNEW it! Do you know how many letters and e-mails I get every day from people who WANT things from me? That's all I ever hear! I want, I want, I want!!!"

"Well, my dear fellow, you are in the business of giving, are you not?" Cattywampus asked. "If we've been misinformed all these years, let me just say that it's hardly our fault, is it? What with popular culture being what it is these days? The messages are all over the place. Buy this, buy that. You can't escape it."

"Stop!" Santa bellowed. "Let me finish! Does anyone ever want to give ME anything?" He jumped up from the desk and flailed his arms around. "No, they never do! It's always gimme gimme gimme," Santa shouted, his face turning purple. "I'm sooooo tired of giving, giving, giving all the time! All I ever do is give! Does anybody ever give stuff to ME? I ask you! The answer is a big fat NO. Nobody ever gives anything to ME." He flopped back down into his chair and mopped his face with a handkerchief.

"Wow. That's some anger you got built up there, big guy," Cattywampus said. "Have you ever thought about taking an anger management class? Or perhaps doing some yoga. I'm a firm believer in yoga to de-stress. I do hours of stretching every morning. And every night. And after every meal."

Santa frowned. "You'd think that just once, somebody would say, oh, Santa works SO hard for us, he slaves away for a whole year, and slogs through snow, and blizzards, and sleet in the darkness of night with only a few measly reindeer for guidance, so surely we should give something back to him. But noooo, that never happens. I'm DONE. Just call me Scrooge Santa, I don't care anymore!" He turned in his chair, crossed his arms and glared.

Cattywampus nodded. "I told you those were reindeer."

Bo stepped forward and whispered to Dot. "Poor Santa. He's lost his heart. He needs a new one. Perhaps we should send him to the Wizard? Remember that story you read to me when I was just born?"

Dot frowned. "Bo, that's not a Christmas story! I'm pretty sure that's a whole different story! Although, from time to time I do wonder…" she admitted.

Cattywampus rubbed his chin. "I know! Why don't we send for the Doctor? I'm sure he can fix Santa's heart. He fixes all sorts of cool things on TV."

"Who?" Dot asked.

The robot whirred. "The doc-tor?"

"Who?" Dot asked again.

"Oh, never mind!" Cattywampus said. "Obviously I'm traveling with a bunch of lowbrows who have never watched BBC."

Finally, Bo cautiously crept forward. "I thought people put out plates of cookies and glasses of milk for you, Santa. Isn't that true, sir?"

Santa stared at the doll. "Who are YOU to question me? Insolent thing. Milk and cookies! A measly glass of milk and a few skimpy plates of cookies! What do you know? You're just a rag doll!" Santa bellowed. "You don't have a brain in your head."

The cat gasped, Bo started sobbing and Dot moved to comfort her.

"Now look what you did! You big old fat bully," Dot said. "You should be ashamed of yourself! She can't help it if she's not very smart."

Cattywampus snarled. "I'll scratch his eyes out! Let me at him!"

Santa's face turned purple. He jumped up from the desk, screeching. "How dare you! Get out NOW! All of you! I don't have time for this!"

Just then, a short elderly lady bustled in. She was dressed in a bright red dress with white furry trim around the collar and cuffs. Little wire eyeglasses perched on her nose. Her hair was sticking out in curly tendrils from a loose bun on the back of her head.

"What's all the ruckus in here?" she asked. She glanced at Santa, took in the situation, and tried to usher the group away from the desk. "I saw on the monitor that we have guests. Hello, and welcome to our workshop. Although, I'm afraid you picked the absolute worst possible time to visit. Come with me, my dears. Mr. Clause is having a bit of a hissy fit today. He gets this way sometimes." She smiled fondly at him and Santa frowned.

Dot's mouth gaped open. "MRS. CLAUSE! There really is a Mrs. Santa Clause!"

Mrs. Clause smiled. "Of course there is, dear! Who do you think manages all the commotion around here? You know what they say, behind every great man, there's a woman!" She laughed and moved over to stand beside her husband.

Santa glared at all of them, but put his head down, hunched over his desk and got back to work, muttering under his breath.

"You'll have to forgive him, poor dear," Mrs. Clause said, patting his back. "He's stressed, and he's depressed. He doesn't think anyone cares anymore. He doesn't know what he's saying! Ever since Rudolph retired he hasn't been the same. He doesn't really mean what he says," Mrs. Clause explained.

"Yes I do! I mean every word," Santa said, glancing up. "It's bad enough I had to lay off over two-hundred elves, then some management consultant talked me into downsizing, outsourcing and mechanizing the workshop and that's been a big disaster. Look at this mess! Nothing has worked right since I outsourced our toys to Mars."

"You outsourced to Mars?" Dot asked. That explained all the boxes she'd seen on the way in.

"Yes, Mars! Where else am I going to outsource?"

"Why would you even do that?" Dot asked.

Santa shrugged. "Those Martians work cheap."

Cattywampus nodded. "Good point. Everybody's outsourcing to save money these days. If you can find a willing group of workers, then hey, why not? Why, I once read an article in the Wall Street Journal that confirmed that very thing! You see it on TV all the time."

Dot glared at him. "You aren't helping."

"He's right, though," Santa admitted. "I'm just about ready to retire and get out of the toy business. Nobody gives a rat's ass anymore," he said.

"Santa! Language!" Mrs. Clause warned. "My goodness."

Dot shook her head. "Well I don't believe this! Listen to all this malarkey. There are lots of people who still care! Lots of little children care, and are anxiously waiting for Santa Clause. And I care."

Cattywampus wrinkled his nose and pointed at Santa. "What a big disappointment you are! After coming all this way, too. I scratch my litter in your general direction from now on!" He turned and shook his tail in Santa's face, taunting him. "I don't know why we even bothered to come here. It's obvious that you're a fraud. And a big old fake to boot!"

Santa jumped to his feet. "Why you scrawny bag of . . ."

"Pfft! Pfft! Rowrrrrrrrrr!" Cattywampus growled, clawing at the air.

Dot pulled him away from Santa.

Santa walked off in disgust. "I'll be in the kitchen, if anyone needs me," he said. "I think it's time for a cocktail. A really big cocktail. With lots of vodka. And a snack. Don't let the door hit you in the ass on the way out."

CHAPTER FIVE

"Wow," Cattywampus said, staring at Santa. "Totally unexpected. And the nerve!" The cat brushed a speck off his fur and nodded at Mrs. Clause. "Good thing you removed me from him. I was about to scratch his little beady coal-like eyes out and punch him in his jelly belly. No wonder Christmas is in trouble, with that attitude!"

Mrs. Clause pulled them aside. "Dot…friends, please come with me. I want to show you something. Now this is top secret. No one must ever find out. Promise?"

Dot nodded. "I promise!"

The cat sniffed. "I shall promise after I see it, then I'll decide whether I shall tell or not."

Bo pointed at the cat. "That's not a real promise," she chided then turned to Mrs. Clause. "I promise!"

"Af-firm-a-tive," the robot wheezed. "I promise."

"Suck ups," the cat muttered. "A whole bunch of suck-ups."

Mrs. Santa smiled. "Remember, you must never tell anyone, especially Santa, what you see in this room."

"OK, OK, why all the suspense? Geez!" the cat said. "Get on with it, will you?"

Mrs. Clause looked around, reached under the collar of her dress and pulled out a key on a long chain. She motioned for the group to follow her down another short hallway. She stopped at a non-descript red door, glanced around then unlocked it. She motioned for them to follow her and they stepped through into a tiny room. She looked both ways then quickly pulled the door shut.

Dot gazed around the little room. It seemed to be some sort of workroom, and it was filled with toys—more toys than Dot had ever seen in her life. It was bright, colorful, homey and cheerful. The buzz of female voices filled the air along with the soft whir of sewing machines and the sound of hammers tapping. All sorts of toys were stacked about and piled on worktables—stuffed dolls and plush animals, toy soldiers, and more.

Dot took it all in. "Wow! Now this is what I'm talkin' about! This is amazing! But…I don't understand. What is this?"

Mrs. Clause smiled. "I call this my Christmas closet. During the year, my friends and I get together and knit sweaters, or sew little dolls, or make wooden toys, and I store them in here. All the ladies of the North Pole Village volunteer to help me make things year round. We figured one day Santa would need a back-up and that day has come. He never looks in here. He thinks it's just a place where I piddle away at my hobbies." She smiled. "Little does he know . . ."

"You may be saving his bacon!" the cat said.

Mrs. Clause smiled. "Exactly."

Cattywampus strolled over to one of the worktables and picked up an intricately painted wooden horse. "This is more like it! These look like REAL toys! Wow, I don't believe this!

Look at the handcrafted workmanship on these!"

Mrs. Clause nodded. "It was the oddest thing. We were getting by just fine for a while with the factory-made toys. A few years ago we started getting a few requisitions for handmade dolls, then other handcrafted toys. The requests for the factory-made toys were all on red or green paper. Then, a few tan ones trickled through. We put the custom requests on tan paper, you see. Pretty soon, there were more tan ones than red or green with lots of custom orders for handcrafted toys. Then, all of a sudden, there were thousands of them!"

"And you didn't expect all the tannish requisitions?" Cattywampus asked, smirking.

Mrs. Clause smiled. "No, we didn't. We were stunned at all the requests for handmade and handcrafted toys. I had a few "moles" planted out on the factory floor, and so I started sneaking these handmade toys in with the others, a few at a time. Now, we get more requests for handmade than the factory-made toys. I'm at the point where I'm going to have to find more help, especially now that Santa downsized the workshop."

The robot wheezed. "I won-dered why there were no elves."

Mrs. Santa looked sad. "Most of the elves were laid off, or 'transitioned' as Santa called it except for a few he retained for security. The others went to other jobs. Most of them work at malls or department stores now during the holidays. A few went on to star in TV specials."

Bo grinned and clapped her hands. "Oh! What a wonderful job that would be!"

"To work in a mall, at Christmas time?" Cattywampus shuddered. "I think that would be the worse kind of hell on earth! All those humans making you work over the holidays. Although, I could definitely get into starring in a TV show!"

"No, silly! That's not what I meant. I meant that it would be fun to work here with all these other toys!" Bo explained.

Mrs. Santa looked thoughtful. "You think so? It takes a certain type to do it well. I certainly love it. My hope is that eventually we'll be able to transition back into all handmade toys. That's really my dream."

Bo looked around, smiling. "Oh, yes, I would love to work here, too! I could design scads and scads of different outfits, and help make new little dolls to wear them! And shoes, and boots that fit!"

I'm never going to live that one down, Dot thought.

"I could certainly use the help," Mrs. Clause admitted, "if you want to stay. You could be my assistant designer."

"Oh, I would love to, but I have to go back with Dot. I'm going to ask Santa to make me into a real little girl," Bo said shyly. "It's what I've always wanted."

"Being real is sooo overrated, you ask me," Cattywampus said, staring at Dot. "Just look at her; she's no happier than we are!"

"Oh, I'm so sorry to hear that you want to go back, Bo. But if you become real, you can't work here with us," Mrs. Clause said.

"Oh, I thought maybe I could come back some day and . . . oh, never mind," Bo said sadly.

Mrs. Clause smiled sadly. "I'm sorry, Bo. Once you leave, you can't come back. But wait, you know what? You don't have to be real to get new clothes! We know how to remove these and make new ones for you. As many as you want! We'll give you a makeover."

"And shoes, too?" Bo asked.

Mrs. Clause laughed. "Yes, my dear. Shoes, too. But I do wish you'd reconsider and stay. We could really use your expertise. Someone with your enthusiasm would be very helpful to me."

Bo looked thoughtful. Or as thoughtful as a doll with a head filled with sawdust can be. "OK then, it's settled. I'll stay here and help you," she decided.

"A tad wishy-washy, are we?" Cattywampus sniffed.

Bo turned to Dot. "I hope it's OK with you, Dot. I'm sorry I won't be going back with you. I have loved every minute I've spent with you. But I'm not happy sitting in a dark, dusty attic. And I don't think I'd be happy as a real girl, either. Mrs. Clause needs me here."

Dot nodded and gave her a hug. "I understand. You do what you think best. I just want you to be happy."

Cattywampus threw his arm to his forehead. "Oh, the agony. The disappointment! I'm soooo disillusioned!"

"Why is that?" Dot asked.

He pondered for a moment. "I thought the North Pole would be like in the cartoons, with lots of little elves singing happily, working at little benches, tapping away at little wooden dollhouses and such. It's been so scaled back, so downsized. What Mrs. Clause is doing is great and all, but geez, it's such a heartbreak. Most of all I thought SANTA would be much nicer to me."

All of a sudden, they heard a huge CLUNK! followed by a horrible, screeching, hammering noise. Then a warning bell clanged.

Cattywampus bushed up his tail and whirled around. "What in the name of Kris Kringle was THAT?"

Mrs. Santa looked worried. "Oh dear! That's not good. That's the warning bell on the mainframe computer. Something's gone horribly wrong! I must go check on Mr. Clause. If something's gone wrong with the main computer now so close to Christmas, he'll have a conniption fit! Quickly, come with me!"

They all raced out of the room, to find Santa.

CHAPTER SIX

They found Santa at his desk, sobbing loudly into his hands. Mrs. Clause rushed over to him. "Oh my dear! What happened? We heard the warning buzzer. Is everything all right?

He looked up and his face turned purple. "No, everything is NOT all right! All of the stupid e-mails crashed the computer! We went on overload status! I got over four billion e-mails today alone, and that poor old machine just couldn't handle them. Just like I said…people wanting, wanting, wanting. I can't deal with it anymore. This old computer can't handle it. I tried everything I know and nothing worked."

Mrs. Clause patted his back. "Oh my dear, is there anything I can do?"

He shook his head sadly. "I need my elves back! I don't know how to fix this thing! I can fly around the world in one night. I can wink and go up a chimney in a split second. I can be in five-hundred shopping malls on the same weekend. I can even fit enough gifts for the entire world into one tiny sleigh pulled by eight tiny reindeer, but I CANNOT FIX THIS CONFOUNDED COMPUTER!"

"Oh my goodness, Santa," Dot said. "That *is* bad."

The robot pulled up to the desk, whirred, clicked and beeped a few times. "Per-haps I might be of as-sis-tance, sir. What seems to be the prob-lem?"

Santa puffed his cheeks. "I haven't the foggiest. If I knew, we wouldn't be in this mess! All of the requests for gifts come through one main terminal and are fed into this computer. Then we print out requisitions for each department. Everything worked much better when requests came in via phone or handwritten Letters to Santa. Now we've tried to switch over so that everything is done by e-mail or text messages. And it's just too much for this old system to handle. There are just too many humans wanting things."

He glared at Dot and she squirmed.

The robot rolled over to the bank of computers and turned slowly from side to side. "I do see some fa-mil-iar tech-nol-ogy here."

"That thing is very, very old," Santa said. "We need to replace it, but now is not the time! I don't see how you can help."

The robot beeped a few times. "Yes, the com-puter is old, but I al-so am very old. San-ta, allow me to as-sist you. I am Mod-el Number Five Four Nine Sev-en dash Three and was de-signed first to be of as-sis-tance to oth-er com-pu-ters. The new mod-els got too in-tell-i-gent and so I was made ob-so-lete and turned in-to a toy. I still have in-ner tech-nol-ogy that can re-pair these old mach-ines."

The cat frowned. "I don't think you should mess around with that, Robot. What if you make it worse? What do you know about fixing computers? You might cause a rift in the space-time continuum and change the whole course of mankind, or in the least, rip a huge gash in the whole fabric of reality."

"Or screw up the Prime Directive," Bo said. "We can't have that! That would really mess up everything!"

The cat stared at Bo. "Now who's been watching too much TV?"

Robot whirred. "Do not be a sil-ly rag-doll. That on-ly oc-curs in bad sci-ence fic-tion mov-ies."

Cattywampus snorted. "Yeah, just like all the talking robots."

Santa glared at the cat then nodded at the robot. "If you can fix it, then by all means, please do so. I'll be forever grateful."

The robot whirred and beeped. "On one con-di-tion."

"Anything! Name it!" Santa said. "You've got me between a rock and a hard place. I'm in no position now to quibble about a few little baubles."

"The oth-ers came here to ask you for things they want. I want-ed a real lit-tle boy to play with. But I rea-lize now that I was not made for that. I was made to work and to as-sist where I am need-ed. It looks like I am nee-ded here for a more im-port-ant job. Perhaps I might be of perm-a-nent as-sis-tance."

"You mean, you want to stay here and work?" Santa asked.

The robot pinged. "Af-fir-ma-tive."

"It sure beats getting tossed into the recycling bin when you're obsolete, doesn't it?" Cattywampus mused.

Santa clapped the robot on the back. "Wonderful! If you can help me get this thing started again, I'll give all your friends what they want. Anything!"

"I know you can do it, Robot," Dot said. "I always thought you were much more than a toy, anyway."

The robot rolled up to the ancient monitor and keyboard and Santa stepped aside. There was a series of loud beeps and whistles, then a small round probe emerged from the robot's chest and engaged with the mainframe. Then it tapped on the keyboard for a moment or two, with no result. The warning bell continued to clang.

Robot tapped again, with no results. Finally, he rolled over to the bank of computers and bashed his head into it, then gave it a huge shove. Immediately, the warning bells stopped and all went silent.

"Oh dear," Bo whispered. "This can't be good."

Suddenly, the computer powered back up with a whir, and a nice steady hum.

The robot turned to Santa. "That should suffice for now. The ma-chine is a-gain in working or-der."

"Wonderful! But what did you do?" Santa asked.

Robot said, "A com-pli-ca-ted ser-ies of ac-tions. Then I re-boo-ted."

"If all else fails, reboot!" Dot said, nodding. "Even I know that!"

The robot asked, "I do hope you have a back-up?"

Santa looked confused, then frowned. "Oh sure, sure. Uh, we do have a back-up, don't we, Mrs. Clause?"

Mrs. Clause smiled. "Oh yes, I have a back up; don't you worry about that. I always keep paper records. The toys will get made and delivered on time this year. Just like always."

"Good! Now, again, what do the rest of you want? I always keep my promises," Santa said.

"Well, all I wanted was an old-fashioned Christmas with my family," Dot said. "And to get back home to them safely."

Santa nodded. "Yes, of course. I think that you'll find it's already been done! Anything else?"

Dot blushed. "Well, it would also be nice to have someone to spend Christmas with. Someone cuddly and soft. But don't tell my mother I said that!"

Mrs. Clause smiled and said, "I think we can arrange that, too, my dear."

Santa turned to Cattywampus. "What about you, my fine furry—albeit strange—friend? What do you want? A new TV, perhaps?"

Cattywampus pranced around in a circle, pulling at his ears. "Oh, there are so many things I want! It's so hard to decide! The pressure! I guess most of all I want to be a real cat. So I can eat fancy foods and wear emerald collars and laze around just being cute. And I want people to fawn over me. AND I want to live with a wonderful family who appreciates me for what I am and puts up with the quirks in my natural nature."

Santa laughed, then nodded. "Spoken like a true REAL cat! Your wish is also granted! Anything else?"

"World peace?" Dot suggested. "I know that's a biggie…"

Santa sighed and shrugged. "I'm working on that one. You humans are a hard lot to deal with. Just as soon as one place goes quiet, another one goes cattywampus."

"Hey!" the cat hissed. "That's my name; don't wear it out."

"Sorry," Santa said. "Couldn't help myself. Anything else?"

"I think that just about covers it, Santa. Thank you so much." Dot hesitated, then pulled Santa into a hug. "Bo was wrong when she said you lost your heart. You just needed to be reminded that you had one."

Santa smiled. "I very nearly came close to losing it, but thanks to you and your strange friends, even I realized what was really important."

Dot turned to say goodbye to Robot and hugged Bo. "I hope you both have fun here and all your wishes come true." She smiled at Mrs. Clause. "I hope your dreams come true, too."

"Thank you, dear. I have no doubt that they will."

"What's she talking about, wife?" Santa asked.

"Never you mind, dear. It's just girl talk," she said.

Dot sniffed, wiped her eyes then turned back to Santa. "Now, how do we get home?"

Santa clapped his hands. "Ah! That's the easiest part of all! I'll take you home myself. Close your eyes now! And you two hold hands…"

Dot and Cattywampus closed their eyes and joined hands to paws. Santa put his finger to the side of his nose, nodded, winked and faded out in a puff of smoke.

Dot thought she heard sleigh bells off in the distance. She felt a rushing sensation, heard a whooshing sound and felt like she was falling. She flailed her arms around and let go of the cat, trying to get her balance, but couldn't. She felt the oddest sensation.

"I'm melting!" Cattywampus said, way off in the distance.

"We're both melting!" Dot answered, then everything faded away in a glitter-sparkled flash of light.

CHAPTER SEVEN

Dot opened her eyes and felt sick to her stomach, woozy and dizzy like she'd had too much to drink. She tried to sit up, but slumped backwards. She blinked and saw her mother and aunt hovering over her, looking very worried. She had an icepack on her head and her feet were propped up on pillows. She was covered with blankets and was lying on the old sofa, back in her mother's living room.

Dot squinted, and took in the scene around her. She blinked, trying to clear her vision.

She heard music. This time, instead of Rockapella, she heard the instrumental strains of *Have Yourself a Merry Little Christmas* drifting softly from the radio. The entire purple and black Christmas scheme has been obliterated. Instead, there were red and green shiny orbs hanging from the wreath over the mantle, bouquets of holly were gathered with bright red velvet ribbons on the side table, and the tree was a model of traditional Christmas with red, green and white Santa Clauses hanging from the boughs. A little red wagon sat underneath the tree, filled with small wrapped gifts, stuffed dolls and toys.

The cardboard manger sat on the mantle, with the chalkware angels and rubber sheep all arranged around it. The tooth-marked baby Jesus figure was displayed prominently in the middle.

Dot sat up slowly, holding her head. "Ouch! Oh, wow, does my head hurt!"

Dot's mother ran to her. "Oh, thank goodness! Dot! Can you hear me? It's your mama. We were so worried about you!"

"She's awake!" Aunt Doris said. "Dot, you just stay put. You had an accident and took quite a bump on your noggin."

"An accident? Where am I?" Dot asked, looking around.

"You're at home, sweetie," Aunt Doris answered.

"What happened?" Dot asked.

"You went up to bed to take a nap, but then you came back down and said you couldn't sleep, so you decided to help your father capture that danged inflatable helicopter. It was blowing all over the neighborhood! It bounced off the Moore's roof, onto the top of the O'Neal's car—you tried to stop it and weren't watching where you were going."

"I don't remember all that," Dot said, rubbing her head.

"You stepped right into the middle of the road. Mr. Parker was backing out of his driveway, gave you a tiny bump, and knocked you plumb over with his VW Bug. Your father saw the whole thing!" Her aunt shook her head. "It's a wonder you weren't killed!"

Her mother nodded. "It's a miracle. You don't even have a concussion, but you do have a heck of a bump on your head. We took you to the emergency room and the doctor gave you some pain medicine then sent us back home. We're supposed to call him in the morning if you aren't feeling better. We came back home and you fell sleep here on the sofa. We didn't have the heart to move you. We've been watching you all night, just to make sure. Don't you remember any of that?"

Dot felt the knot on top of her head and winced. "Not really. I remember going up to bed early, but that's all." She looked around, and frowned. "But I do remember this was different, wasn't it? You changed it in here; all the decorations are different. Everything's different. Wait. . .how long was I asleep?"

"Just a couple of hours, but we got busy," her mother explained. "We finally decided that we'd taken this modern thing a bit too far. We needed to keep occupied instead of just sitting here worrying about you. We took turns watching over you while the other worked on the decorations. We wanted to surprise you."

"Surprise, surprise!" Dot's aunt said, doing her best Gomer Pyle imitation. "Do you like it?"

"Very much! But you didn't have to do this just for me," Dot said, looking around. "It does look great."

Doris smiled at her sister-in-law. "I knew she'd like it!"

"Well, we got to thinking about what you said. You were right. Christmas really isn't the same without all the old memories and little things that make the holidays special. But most of all, it's not Christmas without our family. If something had happened to you, we'd never forgive ourselves."

"I'm so glad you like the decorations. We weren't sure if you would or not," her mother said.

"Yes, I do. I love them! This is everything I wanted. And much more," Dot said.

"These are all the old ornaments and things we found in the attic. We wanted to get all new ornaments that look old, but the store was all sold out."

Dot laughed. "You two are just too much! I'd rather have all these old things anyway. I just didn't want to hurt your feelings. It's perfect. I love it. Thank you."

"Oh, and we got you a real gift!" Aunt Doris said.

"Let me guess—a gift card?" Dot teased.

"Nope. We couldn't wrap this one, though. We wanted to cheer you up when you woke up. We thought you could use some company since, well, since you live alone and all. Unfortunately."

"Mother, please don't start," Dot warned.

Dot's mother smiled and continued. "So you won't be so alone when you go back home." She turned around and pulled a small basket from behind the tree and handed it to her.

Dot heard a series of soft squeaks. She peered into the basket and a tiny, fluffy black kitten with four white paws stretched up and blinked at her with big green eyes.

"We found this little guy at the shelter. Apparently nobody wants to adopt black kittens during the holidays, but we thought you wouldn't mind."

"Oh, mother, a little black kitten! Thank you! He's a perfect gift. I love him!" She hesitated for a moment, gazing at the little fellow. "I think I'll name him Cattywampus Bonaparte," Dot said, wiggling her finger at the small ball of fluff. He reached up and grabbed it, pulling her finger to him.

"Just like your toy cat?" her mother asked, then shrugged. "Why not? That's just such an odd name for such a small creature, but I suppose he'll grow into it."

"I'm sure he will! And I'll feed him fancy foods on a crystal dish!" Dot said, smiling as the kitten snagged her finger with a tiny claw.

"Watch out, you'll spoil him," Dot's aunt said.

Dot nodded and grinned. "That's entirely possible."

"Oh, I almost forgot. Here's a little collar for him. It's got a little green bell. It matches his eyes. This is from me."

"It's lovely! Thank you, Aunt Doris," Dot said, hugging her aunt. "I'm sure he'll love it."

"You'd better watch out," her mother warned. "He's got a temper for such a little fellow. He already took a nip out of my hand."

Dot wasn't surprised at that in the least. She looked around and frowned. "Speaking of the toy cat, what happened to the other toys?"

"What toys, dear?" her aunt asked.

"The old doll, and the robot. And the stuffed cat." Dot frowned. "For some reason, I just thought about them. Just a minute, I have to check something." She got up and quickly climbed the stairs to her bedroom. Her mother called after her, but Dot ignored her. She searched the room from top to bottom. The toys had completely disappeared. She went back downstairs, shaking her head. "I just don't understand it. I had them all right there, beside me. Was it a dream?"

Her mother shrugged. "Was what a dream? I don't have a clue what you're talking about, honey."

"The toys! The old toys," Dot said.

Nancy Lee glanced at Doris and raised her eyebrows. "I haven't seen them since you took them up to your room, dear. Why are they so important now?"

"Mother, you didn't throw them out, did you?" Dot asked, suspicious.

"No! I'd never do that. Not since I saw how attached you still are to them."

"That's right," Doris said. "I haven't seen them since yesterday, either. I assumed you packed them away to take home. Aren't they up in your room?"

Dot frowned. "Well, I did have them, but . . ." She looked around, confused. "They were right there. It's like they vanished into thin air. I just don't understand it." She shook her head. Unless . . . No, her rational mind wouldn't let her believe that it all had been anything else but a dream. But where had the toys gone?

"I'm sure they'll turn up," her mother said. "We're really glad you like the kitten, but we're still working on the world peace thing. We'll start small, and work on family peace. How's that?"

Dot smiled. "I have no doubt that you'll figure it out. Or someone will, eventually. This is all I really wanted. To be at home, with my family. And to . . .wait, what's that I smell?" she asked, wrinkling her nose.

The most heavenly aroma wafted through the air. It smelled like…Christmas.

"Is that another scented candle, or is it real?" Dot asked, sniffing the air. Vanilla sugar cookies were one thing, but Dot hoped there wasn't such a thing as a roasted turkey scented candle.

"It's a real roast turkey! In the oven. Compliments of Mr. Parker. He felt so bad about running you over with his VW," her mother explained. "That old jackass."

"That dear old jackass," her aunt said. "Maybe there's hope for him after all."

Her mother smiled. "You know, he has a son just about your age and I hear he's coming home for the holidays."

"Mother!"

Dot's mother shrugged. "You can't blame me for trying. Herman really is a nice boy, though. I'm sure y'all would get along fine if you gave him a chance."

Dot stared. *Herman*?

"He's kinda short," Doris said, "and very shy, but he's really sweet once you get to know him."

"I think he works in security of some kind," her mother continued.

Dot felt a bit dizzy.

Sleigh bells rang in the distance. Dot's mother looked up. "That must be your father, up on the darned roof again. I'll be so glad when he's finished with the outdoor decorating. He decided to replace the inflatables with something more traditional. He rummaged around in the attic a bit and found some old plywood cut-outs. Remember when we made that set of the eight wooden reindeer?" her mother asked. "If those fly away, we're in trouble!" She laughed.

"If those fly away, then I think we need to cut back on the eggnog," Doris said.

"Are you sure it's Daddy up there?" Dot asked, staring over her mother's shoulder. "Because I'm pretty sure it's not." Her father stood in the hall, dressed in his robe, yawning and scratching his head. Dot caught his eye and he gave her a big smile and a little wave.

"Who else would it be, Santa Clause and his reindeer?" her mother teased, laughing.

Dot blushed. "Well, maybe."

"Honestly, honey, aren't you a bit too old to believe in all that? When are you going to start living in the real world? You and your toys. Honestly, you'd think you were still just a kid."

Dot shrugged, staring at her father. "Oh, I don't know . . . Are we ever too old to believe?"

"That's a very deep question to ponder for another day. After you get some rest. Anything else you need, honey, besides more sleep?" her mother asked.

"No, I'm fine," Dot said, yawning. The kitten crawled up and nestled between Dot's shoulder and the pillow. "I'm perfect. Everything's perfect. Absolutely purrr-fect!" Dot hugged the kitten close to her heart and listened to the gentle sound of sleigh bells ringing in the distance. "I have everything I want," she murmured as she drifted off to sleep.

That night, Dot's dreams were full of nothing but sugarplums.

The End

The Story of this Novella

This story was based on a play I wrote for a competition a few years ago. I wanted to pay homage to the Wizard of Oz, the legend of Santa Clause, and my love for old toys—not to mention play around with a few really bad puns and some pop-cultural references I hope my readers will enjoy. It finally came together in a play titled "Dot and the (Amazing Technicolor) Quest for the Real Santa Clause." Ever since then, I've wanted to turn it into a novella. While I was editing the manuscript, the characters got busy and expanded the story a bit.

I hope you enjoy the heart-warming trip to the North Pole as Dot takes a journey of the imagination with Cattywampus Horatio Bonaparte, the black cat, Bo Raggley, the stuffed rag doll, Robot and the Christmas Fairy.

By the way, as a young woman, I did make a stuffed doll named "Bo Raggley" for one of my nieces. As far as I know, that doll never talked. But she was *always* interested in fashion.

Bobbi A. Chukran, Author

About the Author

Bobbi A. Chukran is a native Texan who writes comedy of all kinds—fantasy spoofs and the "Nameless, Texas" mystery short story series, featuring lots of quirky characters that live in the same town and can't stay out of trouble. She lives in central Texas near Austin with her husband Rudy and a whole herd of cattywampusses.

Other Books by Bobbi A. Chukran

HALLOWEEN THIRTEEN, A collection of macabre and strangely funny short stories
DYE, DYEING, DEAD, A "Nameless, Texas" Murder Mystery Novella
LONE STAR DEATH, A historical Texas murder mystery
THE JOURNAL OF MINA HARKER, A vampire spoof novella & stage play
PRINCESS PRIMROSE & the CURSE OF THE BIG SLEEP, A comedy fairy-tale detective spoof

Published Plays for Youth by Bobbi A. Chukran

LITTLE RED RIDING BOOTS & COOTER COYOTE, MASTER OF DISGUISE
ANNIERELLA & THE (VERY AWESOME) GOOD QUEEN FAIRY COWMOTHER (Brooklyn Publishers).

Keep in Touch with the Author

You can keep up with Bobbi's new books and stories at her writing blog or website.
http://bobbichukran.blogspot.com
http://bobbichukran.com

Please sign-up for Bobbi's customer newsletter. Always fun. And we hardly ever spamalot. Actually, we NEVER spam!
http://eepurl.com/0Jehb

Connect with the author at:

Pinterest:
http://www.pinterest.com/bobbichukran/
Twitter: https://twitter.com/bchukran
Facebook:
https://www.facebook.com/bobbichukranauthor

An Excerpt from PRINCESS PRIMROSE & the CURSE OF THE BIG SLEEP, by Bobbi A. Chukran:

CHAPTER ONE

In the Lair of Moribunda McEvil

Moribunda McEvil lived in an old dusty cobwebby sort of place---the sort of place that you might imagine a witch would live. Her home was so popular with visiting witches that it became the headquarters of SOWWWW, the Society of Wicked Witches, Wizards and Warlocks.

An old table, covered with a messy variety of jars with scritch-scratched labels sat in a corner, and a couple of old wooden chairs sat at either end. A shelf over the table held a motley collection of ancient, dusty spell books.

Moribunda hunched over a boiling cauldron in the middle of the table. She stirred the contents with a long wooden spoon, all the while mumbling to herself. She spooned out a bit, blew on it gingerly, and then took a taste.

"Perhaps just a pinch more woundwort, Eargore? Woundwort is wonderful with elf stew," she said.

Eargore was Moribunda's minion and her faithful sidekick. He had huge ears and he was a wicked spell gone really, really, really bad. Bless his heart!

Eargore took a bite of the elf stew, wiggled his ears and then nodded. "Hmmm. I do believe you are right, Moribunda. A pinch more woundwort, coming up!" He took a jar off the shelf and spooned a tiny bit of grayish powder into the cauldron.

"Perfect, perfect!" Moribunda cackled, stirring the concoction once more and taking another taste. She frowned, shrugged, then took the jar of woundwort from Eargore and dumped the entire thing into the stew.

"If a little is good, then a lot is better! Can't have too much woundwort, can ya now, I always say." She took another taste and smacked her lips. "Now it's really perfect! Time for lunch!" she said as she ladled the mixture out into two bowls.

They sat down to eat and had only taken a few bites when Eargore pricked up his enormous ears.

"I do believe someone approaches, m'lady," he said.

A few moments later, there was a loud pounding at the door.

"Curses!" Moribunda cursed. "This happens every time we sit down to eat! Can't they wait until after lunch? See who it is, and be hasty about it. I can't stand that infernal noise!"

"We could ignore them. Perhaps they'll go away," Eargore suggested.

The knocking at the door became louder, and someone shouted. "Moribunda McEvil! Are you in there? I must see you immediately!"

Moribunda groaned. "Go ahead, then. See who it is."

Eargore rushed to answer the door. "All righty! Keep your knickers on! I'm comin'!" he said.

When he opened the door, Eargore was dismayed to see that the visitor was none other than Snitch, the Tattle-Tale Fairy. Snitch was about as raggedy as a fairy could be. He wasn't very tall, and he wore brown rugged boots that looked like he had trudged through a swamp. His wings were tattered and his tunic was threadbare. He was beside himself with excitement as he swooped his way into Moribunda's home.

Eargore frowned. "What do YOU want? We just sat down to our lunch. Moribunda is much too busy now for visitors. Please call again when it's more convenient for us."

"Sorry, this can't wait! It's urgent," Snitch said.

"Moribunda!" he sang out, ignoring Eargore. "I have news! I'm sure you'll want to know my news. It's the best yet! Am I wrong? Am I ever wrong?"

"Oh, it's you," she said with a frightful scowl. "What could you have to say that would interest me, the most evil wicked witch in this kingdom? And at lunch time, to boot!"

"I'm pretty sure you're gonna want to hear what I have to say!"

"What makes you sure of that, little tattle-tale?" Moribunda asked him.

"Because I have news!" he replied again.

"So you said, Snitch," Moribunda answered, yawning. "But as you can see, we just sat down to lunch, and our brew is getting cold. Please write your news down on a scroll and roll it under the door and I might have time to read it next week. Maybe. If I'm not too busy being wicked and evil!"

With that, Moribunda turned away to leave. Eargore pushed Snitch towards the door.

But Snitch was persistent and pushed his way back in. "This cannot wait until next week! You'll never guess! Come on, guess!"

Eargore wrinkled his nose. "What's this I smell? Something rancid, I believe. Oh, look, it's the little tattle-tale fairy, come to tell tales and stories! With yet more of his earthshaking news. Ho hum. What is it this time, Snitch? Have more toadstools gone missing from the woods? Or maybe there's been an ogre sighting?"

Snitch looked indignant and pulled his tunic down. "Fine then!" he said. "I'll take my tale down to the Tavern in the Woods and tell everyone else. Won't YOU be sorry when you're the last to know!"

Snitch turned to leave, but Moribunda grabbed him by the collar of his tunic. There wasn't anything that annoyed her more than being the last to know the news. And Snitch knew that!

"Oh, all right!" she said. "Fine then! Out with it or I'll curl your tongue so you'll never tell another tale! But this news of yours had better be good!"

Snitch got a cunning look on his face. "Well, you see, this is really big news! But…I'd like to be paid for my work. After all, even a fairy has to eat!"

"Moribunda is not in the habit of paying for news, Snitch. You should know that by now," Eargore reminded him.

"Oh, horseflies! Fine, then. I was just out minding my own business, near the castle, ya know? When I happened to be up on the wall of the tower, looking in the window, and…"

Moribunda interrupted him. "How did you just happen to be up on the tower wall?"

Snitch gulped. "Bird watching?"

"Ha! Continue with your droll little story," Moribunda yawned. "Or should that be troll little story?"

Eargore laughed.

Snitch blushed with embarrassment. "I am not a troll! I'm a fairy!" he exclaimed. "As I was saying, I happened to overhear Queen Floribunda talking with King Rosario. It seems that she was very excited about something, and then she ordered Chester the Jester to have some invites printed!"

Eargore shrugged. "So what? It sounds like the Queen is planning a party. They frequently have balls and sad little affairs and such at the castle. Big whoopee. I do not see why this should concern us."

"Yes, but it's not just ANY party," Snitch confided. "Not an everyday party, at least. She's planning a…"

"…wedding?" Moribunda interrupted again. "I'll bet she's planning a wedding. I suppose one of her handmaidens is getting married. She does so dote on her servants."

Snitch shook his head. "No! Not a wedding….it's much more exciting than a wedding," he said gleefully, bouncing up and down on his pointy toes.

"A jousting tournament, then? I do so love jousting tournaments! Or perhaps a duel?" Eargore lunged and pretended to shoot an imaginary pistol. "I haven't seen a good duel in an ogre's age!"

Snitch shook his head. "No, not those either."

Suddenly, Moribunda reached out and grabbed Snitch's nose and gave it a good tweak. "Out with it, you little tattle-tale! Enough of this dilly-dallying around! I don't have time to waste listening to your tittle-tattle!"

Eargore laughed. "Tattle-tale tittle-tattle! I love it! Good one, Moribunda."

Snitch yelled. "Ow, let go of me nose! All right! I'll tell. The king and queen are planning a birthday party! For Princess Primrose!"

"Who?" asked Moribunda.

"Did I hear you correctly, Snitch?" asked Eargore, frowning.

"You heard me. A party for Princess Primrose," said Snitch.

Moribunda frowned. "I don't believe I know any Princess Primroses. I know a Princess Penelope, and a Princess Petunia, and a Princess Pertrubia and even a Princess Polyantha, but no Primroses. And how old is this new princess?" she asked, staring at Snitch.

Snitch had never seen Moribunda react like this to news before. It was a bit worrisome. He gulped. "She's not exactly what you'd call a new princess. She's been around for a while. I thought you...."

"HOW long, Snitch?" she shouted.

He thought a moment. "I guess she'd be, oh, about fourteen human years now? Surely you know of her. She's your sister's daughter, after all."

"WHAT? Fourteen? Curses!" Moribunda shrieked. "How dare you not keep me informed! How dare my sister have a baby and not tell me! I didn't even know she was expecting! Nobody tells me anything!"

Snitch spoke in a whisper. "I thought you knew about Princess Primrose. I was just going to mention the party. I thought you'd want to know about the party, but... Oh dear, what have I done?"

Moribunda paced the floor and wrung her hands together as she mumbled. "A new little princess, eh? Nobody ever tells me anything around here worthy of mention! This changes things!" She stopped pacing.

"Eargore!" she shouted.

"Yes, madame?" he squeaked.

"Did you know about this child?" she asked him. "The truth, now!"

"Well, um, yes, actually I did, madame," Eargore said with a gulp. "I knew you'd be upset, so I didn't tell you. I'm sorry! Please forgive me!"

Moribunda frowned, then suddenly grinned wickedly. "Hmmm... I wonder if she takes after her Aunty Moribunda?"

Snitch thought a moment. "Well, no, actually, she's quite beee-you-tee-ful! And the king is beside himself with joy and has planted ten acres of red rose bushes for the Queen in honor of Primrose's birthday!"

Moribunda screamed. "Beautiful? I'm ruined! I can't allow a beautiful princess to grow up in my territory. What will the members of SOWWWW think of me? I'll be voted out as president!"

"Who?" Snitch asked.

"SOWWWW! The Society of Wicked Witches, Wizards and Warlocks!" she answered, pacing across the floor. "They'll never let me live this one down! I'll never be able to show my face in the kingdom again. How could I allow this to happen? I'll be ruined by my own niece!"

"Beg your pardon, madame, but we all thought it best not to tell you," Eargore explained. "We've been able to keep it quiet so far. Until this little snitch snitched!"

"How many know about her?" she asked. "Well, tell me!"

Eargore cringed. "The whole kingdom, I expect. Well, everyone but you."

By now Moribunda was pacing back and forth so fast, she was almost a blur. The dust on the floor was raised in a cyclone. Eargore knew that look, and ducked under the table for cover. She started grabbing and throwing things.

Eargore didn't look forward to cleaning up after this.

"And roses! I hate red roses!!! I hope they have big fat thorns on them and she sticks her royal finger! Serves her right! King Rosario never planted roses for me, when we… Oh, never mind! That's all water under the moat---but a new princess! THAT I can't ignore. No matter what, no matter who she is!"

Eargore crept out from under the table and tried to calm her. He knew trouble when he saw it brewing. "With all due respects, madame, you are powerful, but how could you have prevented it? That family of yours is known for poppin' out with beautiful children. There's no way you could have known."

She turned on him. "Oh, stop sucking up, Eargore! The fact is that I'm ruined. Ruined, I say! I'll never hear the end of this. My sister gets to live in the castle with my darling King Rosario, and now THIS? I can't bear it!"

Eargore thought for a moment. "Might I suggest a little…well, a little tweaking with history?"

"What do you mean?" asked Moribunda. "Speak up! My patience is wearing thin!"

"Actually, I'm not sure," he shrugged. "After all, you are all powerful and the most wicked of witches. Surely there's something we can do. Something deliciously evil, perhaps? Or delightfully dastardly?" He rubbed his hands together with glee.

Snitch stepped forward reluctantly. "But…like what? What would you do? You wouldn't actually harm the child, would you? After all, she's your…"

Moribunda interrupted him. "What do you think, Snitch? Why did you come to me, if not to do harm to the child? Why did you even tell me about her? I was fine before I found out. Not knowing was a good thing! But oh, no---you had to snitch. I just can't help myself now. It's not in my evil nature to let perfect opportunities go to waste."

She paced some more, then stopped abruptly. "Eargore! I need some ideas! The spell books! Bring them to me—quickly!"

"Yes, madame! The spell books! Spectacular idea!" He pulled a chair over to the shelf and clambered up. "Let's see what we have here."

Snitch was horrified. "No! NOT the spell books! Please! Anything but the spell books!"

"Ah, yes, here we are. Just the ticket!" Eargore took down a stack of the old books, blew dust off the top one and handed them to Moribunda.

She took the books from Eargore. "It's been ages since I've had to resort to this kind of evil spell. I'm getting a bit rusty," she admitted, leafing through several of the books and tossing them aside. "Hmm, these are worthless! Nothing in this one---nothing suitable. This has to be GOOD! …. Ah ha! Here's a classic! How to Do Away Permanently with a Beautiful Princess, Even if She is Your Niece. Let's see, rose blight, thorns, pricking fingers, noses falling off---ah, here we are! This one is the perfect spell for her!"

Moribunda squinted into her cauldron. "And while I'm at it, I might put a spell on the Queen so that she can't smell those roses! I could do something to her nose....let's see, what can I do?" She continued reading from the spell book, rapidly flipping the pages back and forth. "Ah ha! And here's the perfect spell for them!"

"You aren't going to...kill her, are you?" Snitch whispered.

Moribunda cackled. "Kill my sister and niece? Oh no! Here's the good part! Maybe I'll put them all to sleep for millions of years, then when they do wake up, Floribunda will be an old hag, all wrinkled and gray and very unattractive, and all the rosebushes will be shriveled up! That'll show Floribunda who's the most beautiful! Or, I could do something else. I haven't decided yet! And as for the Princess---well, I don't know exactly what I'll do, but you can be sure I will have something especially evil planned for her."

"I didn't want you to actually hurt her!" Snitch cried. "You wouldn't hurt Princess Primrose, would you?"

Moribunda laughed and it made Snitch's blood run cold. "What would you suggest I do, Snitch? Send them a flowery little greeting scroll congratulating them on the birthday of their precious pretty Princess Primrose? I'm called wicked for a reason, Snitch!"

"Well, I never really thought about it," he admitted.

Eargore nodded. "That's your problem, Snitch. You don't think!"

"Now when is this party? Speak up!" Moribunda demanded.

"Well, I believe it's this weekend. What are you going to do?" Snitch asked.

"Don't you worry yourself what I'm going to do," replied Moribunda. "So, the party's this weekend, eh? Then we have no time to waste!" She clapped her hands, "Eargore, help me gather some ingredients. Quickly now!" She pointed to a page in the spell book. "Let's try this one, shall we?"

He grinned and nodded. "Yes, madame. Delighted to, madame!" He read the spell all the way through and quickly gathered a number of jars together on the worktable. "I will admit I've missed whomping up evil spells and such. It's been ever so long!" he said as he worked. "Just like the good ol' days, eh?"

Moribunda rubbed her hands together. "I cannot wait! And a party! What a perfect time for my evil plan to go into effect! Not only will I eliminate that beautiful princess, I'll also severely tick off my sister the Queen and pay King Rosario back for what he did to me! Everyone will know how wonderfully EVIL I really am!" She cackled and loud thunder boomed through the sky and a fierce wind came up and whistled through the walls of the lair. Lightning crackled and Moribunda cackled. She danced around as she chanted.

"Double trouble, we'll stir up some trouble!

As the cauldron boils and the ingredients bubble!

I'll turn my sister's life into rubble!"

Snitch looked crestfallen. "Oh dear, what have I done now?" he whispered.

END OF FREE SAMPLE

Paperback and E-book available on Amazon.com.
http://www.amazon.com/Bobbi-A.-Chukran/e/B005UK1P7M

www.ingramcontent.com/pod-product-compliance
Lightning Source LLC
Chambersburg PA
CBHW061337040426
42444CB00011B/2972